A GUIDE TO THE JUDAIC ART COLLECTION

OF THE

NORTH CAROLINA MUSEUM OF ART

ABRAM KANOF

North Carolina Museum of Art, Raleigh
1996

North Carolina Museum of Art
2110 Blue Ridge Road
Raleigh, North Carolina 27607-6494
(919) 839-6262

Hours:
Tuesday-Saturday *9:00 AM-5:00 PM*
Friday until *9:00 PM*
Sunday *11:00 AM-6:00 PM*
Closed Monday
Free Admission

The North Carolina Museum of Art, Lawrence J. Wheeler, Director, is an agency of the North Carolina Department of Cultural Resources, Betty Ray McCain, Secretary. Operating support is provided through state appropriations and generous contributions from individuals, foundations, and businesses.

Graphic Design: *Maura Dillon, Magic 8 Design*
Photography: *Bill Gage and Lynn Ruck*

Printed in the United States of America

A GUIDE TO THE JUDAIC ART COLLECTION

OF THE

NORTH CAROLINA MUSEUM OF ART

ABRAM KANOF

CONTENTS

The Judaic art collection at the North Carolina Museum of Art has its origins in a remarkable exhibition of *Ceremonial Art in the Judaic Tradition* presented at the Museum in 1975. The curator for the exhibition was Dr. Abram Kanof, a distinguished professor of pediatrics as well as a recognized authority on Jewish art and symbolism. Prompted by the overwhelming success of the exhibition, the Museum invited Dr. Kanof to oversee the development of a permanent collection of Jewish ceremonial art. He accepted with enthusiasm. By his indefatigable efforts and through the generosity of many North Carolinians, we can now take pride in a collection, unique among American art museums, that nobly celebrates the artistic heritage of the Jewish people. From the day of its opening in 1983, the Judaic art collection has been one of the most popular attractions of the Museum.

This publication answers the multitude of requests for a layman's guide to the Museum's Judaic art collection. Once again, we are grateful to Dr. Kanof. His scholarship and deep humanity are everywhere evident and remain luminous gifts to the Museum and to the people of North Carolina.

Lawrence J. Wheeler
Director

Little of Jewish ceremonial art survives from premodern times. Given historical circumstances, the desire of the Jews to imbue their ceremonies with beauty could not always be satisfied, and such embellishment was not, after all, essential to religious observance. Persecution and recurrent exile — in many instances without notice — discouraged the accumulation and transport of bulky or heavy objects. Generally the Jews carried manuscripts and books describing the ceremonies, rather than the ceremonial objects themselves, into exile. Thus some of the older pieces are known only from a chance illustration in an illuminated manuscript or a rare written description, perhaps in a rabbinical letter or treatise.

The design of Jewish ceremonial objects reflects two forces. One is the uniformity imposed by prescribed religious use. The other is the diversity generated by both the varied national and ethnic influences acting on the far-flung Jewish communities and the era in which the objects are designed. The development of the Hanukkah lamp affords a good example of this interplay. These lamps are ordered creations; the simple requirements — eight lights and a servant light (*shamash*) — suggest a general form. The requirements of ceremonial usage do not change, but in their style, the lamps reflect the time and place of their making. Upon the object's Jewish base environment imposes its influence. For example, the motif of rampant lions is found on both German and eastern European lamps in bench form (cat. no. 30). However, whereas the lions of the typical German lamp are naturalistic and carefully modeled, sometimes supporting a heraldic device, those on Polish and Russian lamps are often executed

in folk style. So marked is the influence of the local style that in many instances one can easily recognize a lamp as coming from Poland, the Netherlands, Italy, or the Near East. The expert can often pinpoint the city and even the craftsman.

Regional influences can also be seen in the container that holds fragrant spices (*b'samim*) sniffed in the *Havdalah* ceremony marking the conclusion of the Sabbath. Many European spice containers are in the form of towers; containers from eastern Europe take the fanciful forms of fish or beast as well as egg, fruit, and flower shapes; in the Middle East, where a fresh myrtle sprig is used, spice containers are rare and usually are in the form of fruit and flowers. The great triumph of the Jewish spirit has been its ability to express itself in a foreign idiom while keeping its inner integrity and ensuring ultimate return to its Hebrew origins.

The earliest cultures to influence the ancient Hebrews were those of the great river civilizations of Egypt and Mesopotamia: the winged cherubs that adorned the Ark of the Covenant were close cousins of the griffins of Near Eastern mythology. The influence of neighboring Phoenicia is evidenced by the fact that King Solomon asked Hiram of Tyre for help in the design and building of the first Jerusalem Temple. Many centuries later, when the synagogue became the focal point of worship, the influence of Greek and Roman temple architecture could be seen; interior arrangements, as required by the liturgy, affirmed the synagogue's Jewish character. Not only architecture, but mosaic floors, vases, and coins reflected the classical influence and even bore images of foreign gods. During the era of the Hasmonean kingdom (164-63 BCE) Judean coins carried emblems borrowed from pagan Hellenistic art; similar borrowings are evident in the ornamentation of buildings and tombs. In Israel, the ancient synagogue at Chorazin shows centaurs and the club of Herakles (Hercules), and the synagogue at Capernaum (Kefar Nahum) has a frieze depicting six cupids. In the synagogue mosaics of Beth Alpha (Beit Alfa), near the scenes of the sacrificial binding of Isaac and of the Temple and its sacred vessels, is a representation of the Greek sun god Helios in his chariot. The mosaic floor of the Nirim synagogue follows the same design as the pavement of the church at Shellal (561 CE) except for the addition of Hebrew symbols.

The wall and ceiling decorations of the third-century synagogue at Dura-Europos in Syria exhibit Greek, Roman, and early Christian influences. A cyclical arrangement frequently used to narrate Scripture is apparent in the wall paintings. This form is borrowed from many Roman and Greek historic reliefs, as well as Greek bowls and vases illustrating lively Homeric scenes. The individual figures at Dura-Europos exhibit a variety of influences. David with his harp curiously resembles the legendary Greek poet Orpheus playing before the angry beasts; it could be Aphrodite, the Greek goddess of love, who rescues the infant Moses from the waters of the Nile; and the rod of Moses suggests the club of the Greek hero Herakles. Other figures are regally posed in the classical manner. Centuries later, both in Prague and in Worms, the figure of Jupiter with his thunderbolt adorned synagogue chandeliers.

(cat. no. 30)

With the passing of centuries, Jews became farther removed from their origins, geographically as well as temporally. Their residence and activities were circumscribed by the restrictive laws of the Christian and Muslim majorities. One result is that the degree of involvement of Jews in craft production differs from land to land. In Europe, the finest gold and silver were made by artisans trained in Christian guilds. Thus, many of the most treasured objects of Judaica are the work of non-Jewish artists. A great deal of work by Jews can best be described as folk art. Indeed, the circumstances of Jewish history and the character of folk art coincide. Unselfconscious and unsophisticated in nature, folk art, for all of its charm, is essentially a village development, largely isolated from high culture and professional training.

In the realm of metalwork, the particular skills that European Jews developed to an almost professional level — despite religious restrictions and outer pressures — included silver filigree, niellowork, and the decoration of pewter. The ancient craft of filigree, a technique in which wires are twisted and soldered into the desired forms, was especially popular from the medieval period onward, chiefly because it was neglected by non-Jewish artisans. Regional differences can be seen in filigree as well. Galician and German filigree tend to be coarse and composed of thick wire coils; Viennese work is very fine, with feathery filaments; Italian work resembles that of the Viennese, but the patterns are more intricate and varied. The decorative effect is sometimes further enhanced by such other means as granulating the wires or placing a pearl or semiprecious stone at the center of the design. From the seventeenth century on, there is a great body of ceremonial objects of all kinds worked in filigree — Torah crowns and finials, mezuzahs, bookbindings, bridal belts, rings, and especially spice containers. The tradition of filigree was revived in the twentieth century by the artisans of the Bezalel School of Arts and Crafts in Jerusalem.

Pewter ware was used extensively for home ceremonials. This material was a favorite because of its malleability and relative cheapness. Pewter objects fall into two groups. The first comprises the ordinary household utensils adapted for ceremonial use — cups for sanctification over wine *(kiddush)*, plates for use at Passover or Purim, and basins for ritual washing of the hands. Decoration with Hebrew lettering and appropriate designs served to transform the mundane into the sacred. The second group of objects is made up of pieces designed especially for ritual purposes, such as Hanukkah and Sabbath lamps and spice containers. Many of these were cast from molds; their wide distribution indicates that these molds circulated freely among pewterers.

It was during the seventeenth and eighteenth centuries that European Jews, particularly in France and Germany, became secure and affluent enough to commission and acquire large numbers of ceremonial objects; hence a great deal of the Jewish ceremonial art of that time adopted the exuberant richness of the prevailing baroque style. Indeed, so great is the power of tradition that the baroque remains a favored style of Jewish ceremonial objects.

The rise of modern functionalism has challenged traditional decoration. The modern synagogue and home favor modern ceremonial objects. Each age has generated its own view of Judaism and has modified its modes of worship, and there is no reason why our age should not produce its own form of sacred accessories. With so many Jewish artists involved in functional and abstract art, it is not surprising that a good many should be attracted to the application of modern ideas and materials in the creation of Jewish sacred objects. Here is a perfect sphere for realizing the modernist ideal of integrating the form of the object with its function and for removing barriers between art and craft, artist and artisan. The Museum's collection is unusually rich in the number of objects in contemporary styles. Insofar as these objects are designed with faithfulness to the use for which they are intended, their form — whether modern or traditional — enhances their sacredness and does honor to the age.

The involvement of Jewish artists in the twentieth century has had an important effect on the design of Jewish ceremonial objects. Gentile artisans could master the forms required in ritual, but only Jewish artists employed the uniquely Jewish elements of elegant calligraphy as well as texts, scenes, and symbols drawn from postbiblical commentaries and liturgy.

Ritual objects such as Hanukkah lamps and spice containers are recognizably Jewish because of their distinctive ceremonial functions. However, how does one identify as Jewish an object that has an everyday use in the secular world — a cup, a wash basin, or a dish? When the form is indistinguishable from that of its secular counterpart, it is often the Hebrew inscriptions and specific decoration that establish an object's ritual status. Even so, it is well to note that a secular form without inscriptions or imagery can still be used in Jewish ritual.

One characteristic of Jewish ritual art is the survival through the centuries of a few fundamental forms and recognizable symbols and motifs. The three main themes in Jewish decoration are those commemorating

(cat. no. 28 – detail)

biblical history, proclaiming the sovereignty of the Torah, and expressing the hope for a just society and the restoration of Zion. The story of the *Akedah*, or Abraham's sacrificial offering of Isaac, is one of the most common biblical motifs. As a symbol of Israel's unwavering faith in God, it is especially poignant during the High Holy Days (hence the story's widespread representation on belt buckles worn with the white robes traditionally associated with those days). The *Akedah* is depicted on many mosaic pavements of ancient Middle Eastern synagogues. It is seen on objects used in the ceremony of circumcision and the redemption of the firstborn *(pidyon ha-ben)*.

Other biblical subjects popular as decorative motifs are Jacob's dream of angels on the heavenly

ladder and his later struggle with the angel; the triumphant passage of the Israelites through the Red Sea; Moses striking water from the rock; the Tablets of the Law (Ten Commandments); Aaron in his priestly garb; Joshua's spies returning with grape clusters from the Promised Land; Samson and the jawbone; David and Goliath; David and his harp; Solomon as judge; Jonah in the belly of the great fish; and Ezekiel's vision of the dry bones brought back to life. As one would expect, objects used in the observance of Passover frequently depict scenes or symbols drawn from the Book of Exodus. Likewise, the decoration of objects for Purim and Hanukkah often is derived from the appropriate biblical sources.

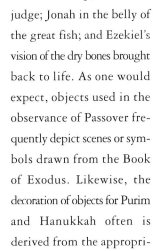

The theme of the restoration of Jerusalem and the Temple pervades Jewish art. It was an especially prominent subject in the centuries immediately following the destruction of the Temple by the Romans in 70 CE. The messianic hope is most commonly symbolized in depictions of Jerusalem, the Temple, and the Temple furnishings.

Sacred utensils, reminiscent of those once found in the Temple, were used extensively to keep alive hope for the future restoration of the Temple: these included the table for the bread offerings (shewbread), the washbasin, and the hand shovel used for the sacrificial ashes. The most ubiquitous symbol was the representation of the original menorah, or seven-branched lampstand, constructed for the desert Tabernacle and later placed in the Temple (Exodus 37:17-24). The rabbis prohibited the making of a duplicate menorah, but its depiction as a symbol was permitted, and as such it is found in every Jewish community throughout the world. The seven-branched lampstand is pictured in ancient mosaics; on the furnishings and decorations of the synagogue; on Hanukkah lamps, seals, medals, coins, wine cups, amulets, and glassware; as well as in sacred manuscripts and books. Placed at the entrance to a house or on a grave, the menorah was, and is, the identifying mark of the Jew and expresses personal as well as national redemption. In our time, the menorah has taken on new meaning as the emblem of the State of Israel.

The form of the seven-branched menorah is thought to have a profound affinity with the ancient Near Eastern concept of the sacred tree. The metaphor of the sacred tree persisted in Jewish tradition: the Torah "is a tree of life to those who grasp her" (Proverbs 3:18); "The fruit of the righteous is a tree of life" (Proverbs 11:30); "Hope deferred sickens the heart; but desire realized is a tree of life" (Proverbs 13:12). God appeared to Abram (later Abraham) at the tree (terebinth) of Moreh (Genesis 12:6), and under this same tree Jacob buried the alien gods of his followers (Genesis 35:4). It is an especially popular decoration on the backplate of Hanukkah lamps, whose shapes accommodate its spreading branches particularly well. In the Christian tradition, it was the crucifixion of Jesus on that "cursed tree" which promises salvation to believers. In illuminated manuscripts of the New Testament,

(cat. no. 28 – detail)

the lineage of Jesus frequently is represented on a tree form, known as the tree of Jesse, because the tree springs from Jesse the ancestor of Jesus.

One of our richest sources of knowledge concerning Jewish symbols and motifs is the ancient Jewish coinage. Much of the Palestinian coinage was minted by the region's Greek and Roman conquerors, but during three periods of Jewish ascendancy or revolt coins carried authentic Hebrew symbols. Under the kings of the Hasmonean dynasty (164-63 BCE) these motifs included lilies, a double cornucopia between pomegranates, the star, the shewbread table, and the menorah. Jewish coinage during the first of two unsuccessful Jewish revolts against Rome (66-70 CE) was distinguished by symbols representing either Temple accessories or objects associated with the Jewish festivals: goblet, pomegranate clusters, wine vessels, vine leaves, a palm tree between two baskets of fruit, the *lulav* (bundle of palm, myrtle, and willow branches), and the *etrog* (citron).

Because they refer to the implements or services performed in the Temple, most of these symbols in the period following the destruction of Jerusalem and the Temple (70 CE) declare nationalist ambitions and the hope for the restoration of the Temple — and Israel. The clustered pomegranates may represent the fruits brought to the Temple as a first offering. Pomegranates have a long history in the art of ancient Israel: they decorated the columns that stood before the Temple of Solomon, and they appeared as motifs on the garments of the high priest. The goblet was undoubtedly a Temple vessel, for it appears on the shewbread table represented on the triumphal Arch of Titus in Rome. The ram's horn *(shofar)* is an especially poignant symbol. It revives the memory of those most solemn moments of the Temple service when it was sounded to usher in the new year. Today it is sounded on Yom Kippur (Day of Atonement) and reminds the synagogue worshipers of the great day when the messiah will be announced with a divine blast "on the great *shofar*." After the destruction of the Temple, representations of the scrolls of the Torah in an ark or shrine became common.

The star within a diadem was adopted by the Jewish king Alexander Jannaeus (reigned 103-76 BCE), probably as a symbol of his kingship. The association of the star with Jewish leadership continued during the First Jewish Revolt and reached its zenith as a symbol during the Second Jewish Revolt (132-135 CE), which was led by Bar Kokhba ("son of the star").

(cat. no. 28 – detail)

The six-pointed star, or *Magen David* ("Shield of David"), though probably the most ubiquitous Jewish symbol in recent times, is by no means the oldest; neither is it rooted solely in Jewish tradition. It was a common decorative motif in the ancient world and as such appeared also in Jewish contexts — on an ancient Hebrew seal and on the wall of the third-century synagogue at Capernaum. The symbol continued as a decorative device in medieval synagogues and on ritual objects. During the same period it took on an amuletic, protective meaning among Jews and Christians and appeared in Jewish texts and on mezuzahs.

It was not until the fourteenth century that the star became identified with the Shield of David,

presumably because the Israelite king was, in legend, reputed to have possessed a magical talisman — a six-pointed star on his shield. Indeed, in medieval times it was the subject of much literary interest, especially in mystic writings. Its first use as an official emblem of Judaism occurred in 1354, when Emperor Charles IV permitted the Jews of Prague to "bear a flag"; when in 1527 Ferdinand I entered the city, the Jews greeted him bearing a flag that featured a large Shield of David. From Prague the idea spread; the residents of several communities in eastern Europe and southern Germany made similar flags. From then on the six-pointed star increasingly gained currency, until it became universally recognized as signifying all things Jewish.

In 1897 the first Zionist Congress chose the six-pointed star as its symbol, thus elevating it to the status of a uniquely Jewish symbol. In Nazi Germany, it was forced as a symbol of shame upon the Jewish people who then poignantly transformed it through suffering into a badge of honor. By virtue of its long association with Jews and Judaism, and despite its non-Jewish roots, the *Magen David* properly became the symbol on the flag of the modern State of Israel.

Other motifs, besides those based on the idea of national restoration, have their origin in national legends, ethical precepts, and common folklore. The zodiac, for instance, was adapted from Roman depictions of the daily and yearly passage of time, and it was a favorite theme in synagogue art during the fifth and sixth centuries. In medieval times the zodiac appeared with considerable frequency in Hebrew manuscripts. In the seventeenth and eighteenth centuries it appeared also in marriage contracts *(ketubbot)* and numerous Hebrew books. (The author can recall the zodiac painted on the ceiling of his father's synagogue in Brooklyn, New York.) The twelve signs of the zodiac may be linked to the twelve tribes of Israel, the twelve loaves of shewbread (Exodus 25:30; compare Leviticus 24:5), and the twelve precious stones in the breastplate of the high priest Aaron (Exodus 28:17-21). Emblems of the twelve tribes also are found. A famous modern example of their use is Marc Chagall's stained glass windows in the synagogue of the Hadassah Medical Center in Jerusalem. According to an old tradition, twelve gates lead into heaven and the prayers of every Jew reach the Almighty through the gate representing his or her tribe.

(cat. no. 28 – detail)

An interesting feature of Jewish decorative art is the use of animals and birds. The lion is the favorite animal motif ("Judah is a lion's whelp"; Genesis 49:9), but the deer also is favored; together with the bird, they exemplify the rabbinic admonition to "be strong as a leopard, light as an eagle, fleet as a hart and strong as a lion, to do the will of your Father who is in heaven." The use of heraldic pairs of fierce animals to guard sacred items is rooted in ancient Near Eastern art. Since the Roman period the lion has been a decorative motif on the Ark of the Law and its related objects. Other notable animal motifs are the bear, the hare, the squirrel, and the ox, often borrowed from the decorative traditions and heraldry of non-Jewish peoples.

Birds have a special place in the Bible and in later Jewish writings. In the Bible, God "mounted a cherub and flew, gliding on the wings of the wind" (Psalms 18:11; see also Deuteronomy 33:26 and 2 Samuel 22:11). The eagle is often represented as hovering protectively over the crown of the Torah, the Tablets of the Law, and the lion of Judah. The eagle has its own messianic meaning. It was especially popular in the decoration of ancient synagogues, presumably reminding worshipers of the promise of redemption: "You have seen . . . how I bore you on eagles' wings and brought you to Me" (Exodus 19:4). In later literature God's chariot is described as being carried through the firmament by winged beings, each with the face of an eagle, a lion, an ox, and a man (Ezekiel 1:6-14). It is important to remember also that the eagle has often been the emblem of the rulers under which

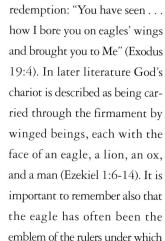

Jews have lived, beginning with the Roman caesars and later including Holy Roman emperors, Russian tsars, Polish kings, and German kaisers. Thus the appearance of the eagle in Jewish art may often imply obeisance to the governing authority.

In Jewish as well as Muslim tradition, as in pagan legend, the soul is often depicted as a bird, and the souls of the righteous, in the form of birds, sit at the throne of the Almighty, singing His praises. Among the feathered creatures that appear in ceremonial art are the dove (symbol of fertility), the peacock (resurrection), the pelican (self-sacrifice), the duck, and the goose.

Fish, another symbol of fertility, also appear. They are especially popular on Purim items, representing Pisces or the zodiacal sign of the month of Adar in which the holiday falls. Fantastic creatures such as serpents with human heads, griffins, unicorns, and dragons also are known. Various fruits, flowers, and leaf motifs are omnipresent in the repertory of Jewish themes. Winged children, a Renaissance interpretation of the cherubim of the Bible (originally griffins), also appear.

A number of symbols of personal identification are used on Jewish ceremonial objects. A pair of hands in the gesture of blessing may indicate that the donor of an object is of priestly lineage; a ewer with basin identifies a descendant of the Temple servitors, or Levites, who washed the hands of the priest. On gravestones the occupation or name of the deceased is sometimes represented symbolically. An example of the latter is the lion on the tombstone of the celebrated Rabbi Loew (Lion) in Prague.

Of all the ornamental elements that grace Jewish ceremonial art, the Hebrew alphabet has the oldest and richest history. One legend has it that Moses arrived in heaven to find God engaged in plaiting crowns for the letters of the Hebrew alphabet on a Torah scroll. According to another legend, God drew the Hebrew letters, hewed them, combined them, weighed them, interchanged them, and through them produced the whole of Creation.

The objects in the Judaic art collection were designed to enhance the ceremonies in Jewish life. They continue a tradition from ancient times when the great Temple in Jerusalem housed a treasury of beautiful ceremonial objects: the Ark containing the Tablets of the Law; the tables with offerings of bread (shewbread) placed in the sanctuary every Sabbath; the ornamental ritual washbasin; the high priest's breastplate, and the various instruments of the sacrificial cult.

Since the destruction of the Temple, the tradition has continued through numerous decorative creations that celebrate Jewish life. The rabbis, now the spiritual leaders of the scattered people, amplified Moses's declaration, "This is my God, and I will glorify Him" (Exodus 15:2) with special illuminations: "Make a beautiful mantle of beautiful silks with which to clothe the Torah."

The collection of Judaica in the North Carolina Museum of Art is divided into four groups. The first consists of objects intended to enhance the beauty and the sacred character of the synagogue. Another is used to celebrate the events of the life cycle. The third group is concerned with the observance of Jewish holy days. The final group contains miscellaneous objects usually found in the home.

THE SYNAGOGUE

The Torah (Pentateuch), consisting of the first five books of the Hebrew Bible, is the central text

(cat. nos. 1 and 2)

in Judaism. It records the story of the Creation and the ancient history of the Jewish people and outlines the basic tenets of Jewish personal and communal conduct. It is chanted to the congregation in prescribed sections during the Saturday morning prayers; shorter sections are read on Monday and Thursday mornings and on certain festivals and holidays. Highly trained scribes precisely copy the words of the Torah onto scrolls of parchment or fine leather. The scrolls are undecorated; their beauty depends on the precision and elegance of the calligraphy, which has remained unchanged for centuries. In the Ashkenazi (European) tradition, the scroll is wound on two rods or staves. After the reading, the two staves are brought together and joined with a binder. The Torah is then sheathed in a mantle to protect and sanctify it and finally returned to the Ark in the east wall of the sanctuary.

The staves that protrude through the top of the mantle are decorated with a pair of finials *(rimmonim)* or a crown *(keter)*. There are two basic forms of finials: the tower, the earliest extant form and prevalent in Europe (cat. no. 3), and the fruit form, often made in the shape of a pomegranate (cat. no. 2) — *rimmonim* literally means "pomegranates." The pomegranate is one of the seven biblical fruits of the Holy Land (the others being the grape, fig, olive, date, wheat, and barley). Traditionally, the pomegranate contains 613 seeds — the number of commandments in the Torah. The finials as well as the crowns may be adorned with tiny bells, which audibly herald the procession in which the Torah is carried through the synagogue before being read; they also recall the bells on the garment hems of the high priests in the ancient Temple.

The crown, or *keter*, symbolizes the sovereignty of the Torah. The Torah crowns are distinguished from royal crowns by their decoration, which can include animal and plant forms, the menorah, and other objects associated with the Jerusalem Temple. One of the Museum's Torah crowns (cat. no. 4) is surmounted by a tree of life. A modern Israeli crown is of bent silver rods with pearls substituting for the traditional bells (cat. no. 5).

The Torah is further adorned by two items that hang by silver chains from the protruding staves. The first of these is the shield, or breastplate *(tas)*, usually made

(cat. no. 4)

of silver. Its primary function is to identify the specific occasion on which the scroll is to be read. One of the Museum's shields (cat. no. 6) is decorated with heraldic lions supporting the crowned Tablets of the Law (Ten Commandments). A modern Torah shield (cat. no. 7) features twelve enamel tiles that recall the twelve stones on the breastplate of the high priest of the ancient Temple, which themselves symbolized the twelve tribes of Israel. The encircling inscription refers to the Thummim and Urim, mysterious objects placed in the breastplate of the high priest and used as a medium for the revelation of God's will. The second item hung around the staves is the pointer *(yad)*, which generally is configured in the shape of a pointing hand (cat.

no. 8). The pointer is used to guide the reader as the Torah is being read.

When the two parts of the scroll are tightly rolled and bound together, the mantle drawn over it, the protruding staves decorated with crown or finials, and the shield and pointer hung from the staves, the Torah is considered fully dressed in accordance with the traditions of the Ashkenazi Jews of Europe. The Torah on display in the gallery, however, is dressed in the manner of the Sephardi Jews,

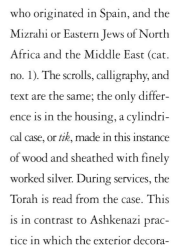

who originated in Spain, and the Mizrahi or Eastern Jews of North Africa and the Middle East (cat. no. 1). The scrolls, calligraphy, and text are the same; the only difference is in the housing, a cylindrical case, or *tik*, made in this instance of wood and sheathed with finely worked silver. During services, the Torah is read from the case. This is in contrast to Ashkenazi practice in which the exterior decorations are completely removed and the scroll unrolled onto a flat table for reading.

The hanging oil lamp, the *ner tamid*, or eternal light (cat. no. 9), is always hung in front of the Ark that houses the Torah. Reminiscent of the lamp that burned continuously in the ancient Temple, it symbolizes the eternal presence of God.

One of the more impressive objects in the collection is the large bronze plaque, or *mizrah* (cat. no. 10), which was hung in the synagogue to indicate the direction for prayer. Traditionally, Jews pray facing east, in the direction of the ancient Temple. This plaque depicts the stone walls and the twin columns of the Temple as well as heraldic lions, birds, and the crown of Torah.

THE LIFE CYCLE

Besides the rituals that are a part of the daily life of an observant Jew, other ceremonies celebrate milestones throughout the life cycle. The most important of these events are birth, *bar/bat mitzvah*, marriage, and death. All of these ceremonial observances focus upon the covenant between God and the Jewish people.

The birth of a boy is marked by a circumcision ceremony, or *brit milah*. The term means "covenant of circumcision." By undergoing circumcision a boy enters into the ancient covenant first made by God with Abraham (Genesis 17:9-14). The *brit milah* takes place when a baby is eight days old and is performed by a *mohel*, who in the past might have used instruments as seen here in our set (cat. no. 11). One side of the flask containing astringent powder depicts the *Akedah*, or Abraham offering the sacrifice of his son Isaac. The knife handle is embossed with the standing figures of Moses the Lawgiver and Aaron the High Priest. For firstborn males who are not descendants of the Temple priests and servitors, a second ritual, called the *pidyon ha-ben*, takes place one month after birth. At this ritual the child is relieved of the ancient obligation to serve in the Temple. The obligation to redeem the firstborn also derives from the story of the Passover when the Israelites were spared from the slaughter of the firstborn Egyptian sons (the tenth plague). The child is often carried to the ceremony on a large plate. The Museum's plate (cat. no. 12) is appropriately decorated with the scene of the finding of the infant Moses. As recounted in Exodus, the daughter of Pharaoh discovers the child in a wicker basket beside the Nile River. The artist, probably inspired by a print or painting, set the biblical drama in seventeenth-century Europe.

At age thirteen, each boy becomes fully responsible for the performance of all aspects of religious life and for the fulfillment of the religious duties of a Jewish adult. At this time, the *bar mitzvah* (literally "son of the Commandment") is given the privilege of reading from the sacred Torah scroll before the congregation. In the Conservative and Reform traditions, a girl is honored in a similar ceremony as a *bat mitzvah* ("daughter of the Commandment").

Marriage is the next important step in the Jewish life cycle. The Hebrew word for marriage is *kiddushin*, which means sacredness or sanctity, thus emphasizing the holiness of the vows. The ceremony is performed under a canopy, symbolic of the first roof under which the couple will live together. The marriage ceremony is rich in ritual and highlighted by the reading of the *ketubbah* or marriage contract. By it the groom undertakes to provide for his wife in case of death or divorce. The document is often decorated with biblical scenes sometimes related to the names of the couple as well as scrolls, animals, geometric patterns, and allusions to happily married life. The Museum's example (cat. no. 13) comes from the Sephardic community in Morocco. The standard Hebrew text is inscribed within a conventional architectural format, together with flowers and pairs of fish and birds — perhaps expressive of love, fidelity, and long life for the couple. Presentation of a ring by the groom to the bride is an important part of the ceremony. The Museum's ring (cat. no. 14) is comparatively simple. Other rings are quite elaborate, often decorated with a representation of a happy home. Sometimes the wedding gifts include a ceremonial belt for the bride (cat. no. 15). Although not exclusively Jewish, such adornments symbolize womanhood.

The ritual preparation of the deceased for burial is very complex and is carried out by a volunteer burial society called a *hevra kaddisha* (literally "holy fellowship"). The fellowship observes the anniversary of the death of Moses, a day of fasting and penitential prayers that ends with a banquet and toasts from a ritual cup. The Museum's silver and ivory goblet (cat. no. 16) depicts two events in the life of Moses: the finding of the infant by the daughter of Pharaoh and her attendants and the giving of the Tablets of the Law to the Israelites. Donations to charity are part of every funeral. The Museum has an unusual alms container in the form of a synagogue (cat. no. 17) with a slot for coins and a lidded compartment, presumably for paper currency. One of the inscriptions reminds mourners that "righteousness *(charity)* saves from death."

(cat. no.18)

HOLIDAYS AND FESTIVALS

Most Jewish ceremonies are home events. The most important holy day is the Sabbath, a day of rest in obedience to the often-repeated biblical commandment: "Six days shall you work, but on the seventh day you shall cease from labor" (Exodus 34:21). The Sabbath commences on Friday evening in the home when the mother pronounces the prescribed benediction, lights the candles, and confers her blessing on her children. It ends on Saturday night with a ceremony *(Havdalah)* that incorporates the senses: the lighting of candles, the sipping of wine, and the inhaling of the fragrance of sweet herbs from a spice container — this to carry the sweetness of the Sabbath into the week ahead. The Museum's Sabbath objects include a pair of traditional silver candlesticks decorated with heraldic lions (cat. no. 18) and a modern candelabrum (cat. no. 19) as well as a variety of spice containers, both traditional and modern (cat. nos. 20-23). A contemporary Israeli design combines candlestick, wine cup, and cylindrical spice containers into an elegant *Havdalah* set (cat. no. 24).

The most colorful and family-centered of the holy days is Passover *(Pesah)*, which commemorates the liberation of the Israelites from bondage in Egypt and affirms confidence in the eventual messianic redemption. The celebration takes the form of a service, or seder, centered around the family table. There are prescribed prayers and the retelling of the story of the Exodus, set down in a book, the Haggadah. There follows a festive meal, which commonly ends with song. Passover celebrates the sweetness of freedom while at the same time recalling the bitterness of slavery, each symbolized by appropriate foods: horseradish (bitterness); haroset, a mixture of fruit, nuts, and wine (the sweetness of freedom); lamb shank (sacrifice); and egg (life). These are usually served on a large plate set before the person leading the seder. The pewter plate (cat. no. 25) depicts the four sons of the traditional Passover narrative: the wise one, the wicked one, the simple one, and the one who does not know how to ask. Each personifies a different religious attitude. Around the rim of the plate is inscribed in abbreviated Hebrew the order of the seder:

Sanctification over wine

Washing the hands

Dipping the greens

Dividing the middle portion of unleavened bread (matzah)

Narrating the Passover story

Washing the hands

Blessing bread

Blessing the matzah

Eating the bitter herb (maror)

Wrapping the maror *with* matzah

Serving the meal

Eating the concealed afikomen (matzah)

Reciting the Grace after meals

Praising the Lord

Concluding the service

The modern silver plate (cat. no. 26) illustrates scenes of preparation for the seder. Even more striking in its modernist design is a seder set (cat. no. 27) incorporating tiered plates for *matzah* with dishes and a wine cup. Wine is drunk during the meal, and traditionally a cup is provided for the prophet Elijah, who is said to visit the seder of every Jew and will one day usher the messiah into Jerusalem. The Museum collection includes two Elijah cups, one traditional (cat. no. 28) with figures of the four sons, and one modern (cat. no. 29).

Hanukkah celebrates the successful uprising of the Jews against Seleucid (Hellenistic) domination led by Judah the Maccabee, which culminated in 164 BCE with the conquest of Jerusalem. The victorious Jews then re-dedicated the Temple by renewing the altar and seven-branched lampstand or menorah. According to tradition, they found only a small amount of uncontaminated oil with which to rekindle the lamps. Miraculously, the oil lasted eight days, the length of time needed to purify new oil. Jews annually commemorate the re-dedication by light-

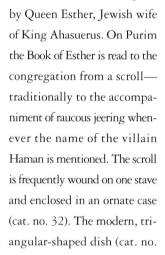

(cat. no. 32)

ing a Hanukkah lamp with candles or oil receptacles for eight successive nights. The menorah form with eight lights is generally used in synagogues (cat. no. 30), whereas smaller versions and bench-type lamps (cat. no. 31) are used in homes. The filigreed back of the Museum's bench-type lamp is decorated with the crowned Tablets of the Law, supported by lions.

Another historically based festival is Purim, which commemorates the rescue of the Persian Jews by Queen Esther, Jewish wife of King Ahasuerus. On Purim the Book of Esther is read to the congregation from a scroll—traditionally to the accompaniment of raucous jeering whenever the name of the villain Haman is mentioned. The scroll is frequently wound on one stave and enclosed in an ornate case (cat. no. 32). The modern, triangular-shaped dish (cat. no. 33) is used during the Purim festivities for serving sweet delicacies to friends, a custom derived from the biblical story. The green of the inset stones alludes to Persia.

The harvest holiday of *Sukkot* is one of three biblical pilgrimage festivals during which Jews "ascended" into Jerusalem in the days of the ancient Temple. (The other two are Passover and *Shavuot*, which celebrates the giving of the Law to Moses on Mount Sinai.) *Sukkot* means "booths," connoting the desert shelters of the Israelites in the wilderness, and during the seven days of this holiday Jews live in huts, where they take their meals "in order that future generations may know that I [God] made the Israelite people live in booths when I brought them out of the land of Egypt" (Leviticus 23:43). During *Sukkot*, prayers are said over a bundle of palm, myrtle, and willow fronds and over an *etrog*, or citron. The *etrog* is often kept in a decorative bowl or container (cat. no. 34).

The *shofar* (cat. no. 35), or ram's horn, is blown during the solemn services of the High Holy Days — Rosh Hashanah (New Year) and Yom Kippur (Day of Atonement). It recalls the horn sounded from heaven upon Mount Sinai at the announcement of the Tablets of the Law (Exodus 19:16). Traditionally, it will be heard again throughout the world at the arrival of the messiah. The *shofar* generally is free of ornament except for carved designs or Hebrew inscriptions. Another interesting object associated with the holidays is the silver filigree bouquet (cat. no. 36). Filled with fragrant spices, it was carried by a well-to-do Polish woman to sustain her through the long religious services of the High Holy Days.

THE JEWISH HOME

Judaism is a religion that, to a large degree, centers on the home and the family. Many religious objects, therefore, are designed specifically for the house.

The Jewish home is identified at its entrance by a small object called a mezuzah, which is attached to the doorpost (cat. nos. 37, 38). The mezuzah is a case containing a parchment on which are inscribed the cardinal principles of faith: "Hear, O Israel! The Lord is our God, the Lord alone. You shall love the Lord your God with all your heart and with all your soul and with all your might" (Deuteronomy 6:4-9). It is not a magical charm. It serves to remind Jews of their duties as they go out into the world each day. The case can be made of metal, wood, textile, or ceramic and varies from simple to elaborate in design.

Frequently the case has a window though which one can see on the parchment the Hebrew word *shaddai*, which means Almighty, or else the case bears the word or its initial letter. For many centuries, Jews entering a new town could find a place to stay by looking for a mezuzah on the doors of strangers.

Often the most distinctive feature of the Jewish home is its library. Traditionally, study rates as high as prayer as a means of worship. Illustrated books and manuscripts have survived the vicissitudes of flight and exile much better than have the sacred objects, and they are prized above all other possessions of the Jewish family (cat. no. 39).

Every Jewish home has a charity box, which traditionally is honored by the wife, who drops in a coin or two as she approaches the Sabbath table. The Museum's example (cat. no. 40) is of a contemporary design.

The Jewish year and life cycle are marked by many holidays, all of which are glorified by the use of ceremonial objects. This embellishment is formalized by rabbinical dictum. These objects, together with the objects in the synagogue as well as those used in daily and communal rituals and functions, form the essence of Jewish ceremonial art. That some of these traditional pieces or their prototypes were made by non-Jewish artisans does not deny their Jewishness. If used in a Jewish context, the object is Jewish. More than a celebration of the art of a particular religion, the Judaic art collection of the North Carolina Museum of Art addresses the universal relationship between religious belief and artistic imagination.

1. *and* 2.

NOTES:

Only important and/or interesting inscriptions are translated.

Biblical passages and citations follow the translation authorized by the Jewish Publication Society, 1985.

Dimensions: H=*height*, W=*width*, D=*depth*, and DIAM=*diameter*.

THE SYNAGOGUE

1.

Torah Case *(Tik)*

1908 (per inscription)

North Africa

Silver: die-stamped, repoussé, cast, appliqué, chased, engraved, partially gilt; wood; textile

H 36-7/8 in. (93.7 cm.), DIAM 10-1/2 in. (26.7 cm.)

Inscriptions (Hebrew): *This case and Torah scroll within it are dedicated by the great lady Dina, most blessed of women in the tent* (Judges 5:24), *wife of Rafael Aharon, sexton, in the year 5668 (1908 CE). Permission is given to the synagogue by the donors to move this Torah wherever necessary. This is the Teaching that Moses set before the Israelites* (Deuteronomy 4:44). *These are the laws, rules, and instructions that the Lord established* (Leviticus 26:46). *Dedicated to the soul of the righteous woman, may glory rest upon her, Dina, the daughter of Hannah, may she be remembered always, who has gone to her eternal home, Sunday, the twelfth day of Kislev, in the year 5692 (26 November 1931). May her soul be bound up in the bonds of eternal life.*

Judaic Art Fund and Museum Purchase Fund

80.3.5

2.

Pair of Torah Finials *(Rimmonim)*

18th-19th century

Middle East, possibly Yemen

Brass: hollow-formed, chased

Each: H 10-1/8 in. (25.7 cm.)

Judaic Art Fund and Museum Purchase Fund

80.3.6a-b

3.

4.

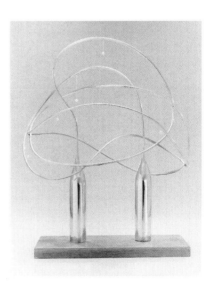

5.

3.

Pair of Torah Finials *(Rimmonim)*

Early 19th century

The Netherlands

Silver: hollow-formed, filigree, cast

Each: H 13-1/2 in. (34.3 cm.)

Gift of David Falk

76.4.1a-b

4.

Torah Crown *(Keter)*

19th century

Poland

Silver: die-stamped, repoussé, chased, cast,

partially gilt; brass: hollow-formed, turned

H 12-5/8 in. (32.1 cm.), DIAM (rim) 7-5/8 in.

(19.4 cm.)

Gift of Mr. and Mrs. Gordon Hanes, in loving

memory of Herbert Brenner

80.6.1

5.

Torah Crown *(Keter)*

1959

Moshe Zabari (Israeli, born 1935)

Silver: hollow-formed; pearls

H 17-1/2 in. (44.5 cm.), W 15-1/8 in. (38.4 cm.)

Gift of Dr. Naomi M. Kanof in memory

of Max Tendler

77.3.3

6.

7.

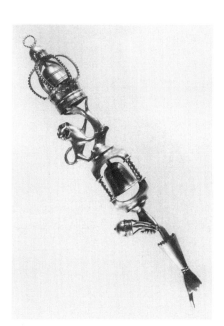

8.

6.

Torah Shield *(Tas)*

1807 (per hallmark)

Central Europe, possibly Bohemia

Silver: die-stamped, chased, engraved, partially gilt

H 14-7/8 in. (37.8 cm.), W 13 in. (33.0 cm.)

Note: inscribed on the two tablets is the standard Hebrew abbreviation of the Ten Commandments; the slot below is fitted with interchangeable plaques designating the day on which the Torah is to be read (in this case *shabat*, the Sabbath); on the cartouche at the bottom is a later French and Hebrew dedication.

Judaic Art Fund and Museum Purchase Fund

80.3.3

7.

Torah Shield *(Tas)*

1975

Ludwig Yehuda Wolpert (American, born Germany, 1900-1981) and Chava Wolpert Richard (American, born Germany 1933)

Silver: pierced, engraved; copper; enamel

DIAM 8-1/2 in. (21.6 cm.)

Inscription (Hebrew): *Let Your Thummim and Urim be with Your faithful one* (Deuteronomy 33:8).

Gift of Dr. and Mrs. Morton Pizer and their children, in memory of Dr. and Mrs. Selig B. Kousnetz

78.13.1

8.

Torah Pointer *(Yad)*

Mid-19th century

Bohemia (Prague)

Silver: hollow-formed, cast, chased

L 11 in. (27.9 cm.)

Gift of Dr. and Mrs. Ronald H. Levine

76.4.2

9.

10.

11.

12.

9.

Eternal Light (*Ner Tamid*)

18th century

Iraq

Glass: painted

H 11-1/2 in. (29.2 cm.), D 8-1/4 in. (21.0 cm.)

Inscription (Hebrew): *To the eternal rest of the sage and wise man, the holy Rabbi Samuel Bibas, may his memory be for blessing, son of the holy Rabbi Joseph ..., who went to his eternal home on the first day of the week of the new moon, in the month of Kislev, in the year 5608 (1848 CE). May his soul be bound up in the bonds of eternal life.*

Purchased with funds from the Hanes Corporation

77.15.1

10.

East Wall Marker (*Mizrah*)

c.1900

Poland

Brass: repoussé, chased, patinated

H 31-5/8 in. (80.3 cm.), W 23 in. (58.4 cm.)

Inscriptions (Hebrew): *Know before Whom you stand, before the King of Kings, the Holy One, praised be He* (Babylonian Talmud, Brachot 25b). *I am ever mindful of Your Presence* (Psalms 16:8).

Judaic Art Fund and Museum Purchase Fund

80.3.4

11.

Circumcision Set with Knife, Powder Flask, and Pincers

20th century

The Netherlands

Silver: hollow-formed, repoussé, cast, chased, engraved

Knife: L 3-13/16 in. (9.7 cm.); flask: L 3-5/8 in. (9.2 cm.), W 2-7/16 in. (6.2 cm.); pincers: L 2-1/2 in. (6.4 cm.)

Gift of Mr. and Mrs. Albert List

76.4.7a-c

12.

Plate for the Ceremony of *Pidyon ha-Ben* **(Redemption of the Firstborn Son), with Scene of the Finding of the Infant Moses**

19th century

Germany

Silver: repoussé, engraved, chased

L 19-1/4 in. (48.9 cm.), W 23-1/4 in. (59.1 cm.)

Inscription (Hebrew): *This is my son, first born of his mother. The Holy One, praised be He, has commanded to redeem him, as it is written in the Torah: "When he is one month old you shall redeem him for five shekels."*

And it is written: "Consecrate unto Me every firstborn of Israel; he is Mine" (Liturgy). *Take as their redemption price, from the age of one month up, the money equivalent of five shekels by the sanctuary weight, which is twenty gerahs.* (Numbers 18:16). *Consecrate to Me every firstborn; man and beast, the first issue of every womb among the Israelites is Mine* (Exodus 13:2).

Judaic Art Fund and Museum Purchase Fund

80.3.2

13.

28

13.

Marriage Contract *(Ketubbah)*

1870 (per inscription)

Morocco (Tetuan)

Tempera and ink on parchment

L 18-1/4 in. (46.4 cm.), W 14-1/8 in. (35.9 cm.)

Note: the Aramaic text is standard for marriage contracts. The couple are Yomtov son of Shatrit and his bride Miriam. The document is dated 5630 (1870 CE)

Purchased with funds from Temple Beth El, Wilson, N.C., and the Hanchrow family, in memory of Joseph H. Hanchrow

82.9

14.

16.

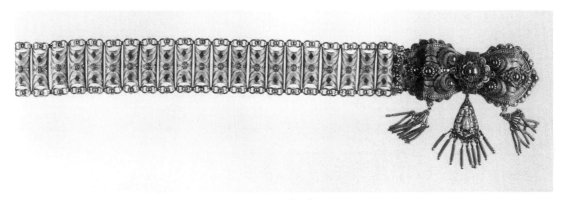

15. *detail*

14.

Wedding Ring

19th century

North Africa

Gold: cast, granulation, appliqué

DIAM 13/16 in. (2.0 cm.), L 1-1/8 in. (2.9 cm.),

W 5/8 in. (1.6 cm.)

Inscription (Hebrew) inside ring: *Good luck*

(mazel tov).

Given by Dr. and Mrs. William Jasper in honor

of Mary Friedman

82.7

15.

Bridal Belt

19th century

Middle East, possibly Yemen

Silver: filigree, partially gilt

L 29-1/8 in. (74.0 cm.); W 1-1/2 in. (3.8 cm.)

Gift of Elizabeth F. Gervais-Gruen, in honor of the

marriage of her son Robert A. Gruen

95.11

16.

**Burial Society Cup Depicting Two Scenes
from the Life of Moses**

1895 (per inscription)

Probably Germany

Ivory: carved; silver: hollow-formed, cast, chased,

engraved

H 15-1/8 in. (38.4 cm.), DIAM (rim) 4-1/4 in.

(10.8 cm.), DIAM (base) 5 in. (12.7 cm.)

Inscription (Hebrew) on lid: *The Holy Congregation,*

(town unidentified), *in the year 5656 (1895 CE),*

according to the counting.

Gift of the Hanes Corporation

77.15.2

17.

18.

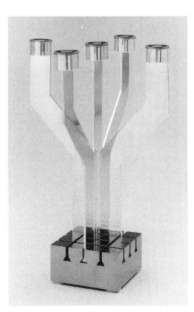

19.

17.

Alms Container in the Form of a Synagogue

1839/40 (per inscription)

Austria

Silver: engraved, chased, cast, appliqué

H 8-1/4 in. (21.0 cm.), W 7-1/8 in. (18.1 cm.),

D 6-3/4 in. (17.1 cm.)

Inscriptions (Hebrew): *Righteousness (charity) saves from death* (Proverbs 10:2). *A gift in secret subdues anger* (Proverbs 21:14). *The House of the Society of Burial and Deeds of Loving Kindness, The Holy Congregation of Salzburg (the capital), in the year 5600 (1839/40 CE).*

Translation of German inscription: *For the widow.*

Gift of the Hon. and Mrs. Marshall A. Rauch

78.15.2

HOLIDAYS AND FESTIVALS

18.

Pair of Sabbath Candlesticks

Mid-19th century

Germany

Silver: cast, die-stamped, chased, engraved

Each: H 8 in. (20.3 cm.),

DIAM (base) 3-3/4 in. (9.5 cm.)

Purchased with funds given by family and friends in memory of Dr. Frances Pascher Kanof

89.1/1-2

19.

Sabbath Candelabrum

1987

Yaakov Greenvurcel (Israeli, born 1952)

Silver: machine cut; brass: machine cut, turned, gold-plated

H 12 in. (30.5 cm.), W 8-7/8 in. (22.5 cm.),

D 8-3/4 in. (22.2 cm.)

Purchased with funds from Dennis J. Winner, Robert I. Winner, and Leslie J. Winner in memory of their father, Harry Winner

88.1

20.

21.

22.

20.

Spice Container in the Form of a Tower
Late 19th century
Eastern Europe
Silver: filigree, hollow-formed
H 10-1/16 in. (25.6 cm.), DIAM (base) 2-1/8 in.
(5.4 cm.)
Gift of Mrs. Rudolf Gumpert
76.22.1

21.

Spice Container in the Form of a Tower
1899 (per hallmark)
Poland
Silver: filigree, partially gilt
H 8-15/16 in. (22.7 cm.), DIAM
(base) 1-15/16 in. (4.9 cm.)
Gift of Elizabeth F. Gervais-Gruen in
honor of S. Daniel Gruen
96.1.3

22.

Spice Container in the Form of an Egg
19th century
Central Europe
Silver: cast, repoussé, chased; wood, carved
H 6-1/8 in. (15.6 cm.),
DIAM (base) 3 in. (7.6 cm.)
Gift of Elizabeth F. Gervais-Gruen in honor of
David Jonathan Gruen
96.1.2

26. *(See page* 39*)*

24.

23.

23.

Traveling Spice Container in the Form of a Book
Late 19th century
Germany (?)
Silver: hollow-formed, chased, pierced, appliqué
L 2-1/2 in. (6.4 cm.), W 3-13/16 in. (9.7 cm.),
D 5/8 in. (1.6 cm.)
Inscription (Hebrew): [Blessed be the Lord]
Who creates a variety of sweet spices.
Gift of the Ideal Fastener Corporation
78.3.1

24.

Havdalah **Set** (spice containers, wine cup and candlestick)
1968
Moshe Zabari (Israeli, born 1935)
Silver: hollow-formed, turned, pierced; walnut
H 5 in. (12.7 cm.), W 13 in. (33.0 cm.),
D 3-5/8 in. (9.2 cm.)
Inscriptions (Hebrew) on handles: *From sacred.... to secular.*
Gift of Mr. and Mrs. Leslie Fuchs
77.3.4 a-d

25.

Passover Seder Plate
18th century
The Netherlands
Pewter: chased, engraved
DIAM 15-1/4 in. (38.7 cm.)
Note: inscribed in Hebrew around the rim is the order of the seder service; the four sons of the traditional Passover narrative are also identified.
Judaic Art Fund
76.4.5

25. *(See page 37)*

27.

26.

Passover Seder Plate

c. 1952-1955

Ilya Schor (American, born Poland, 1904-1961)

Silver: hollow-formed, pierced, chased, repoussé, engraved, appliqué

DIAM 17 in. (43.2 cm.)

Inscription (Hebrew): *It is this promise that has sustained our ancestors and us; for not just one enemy has arisen to destroy us; rather in every generation there are those who seek our destruction, but the Holy One, praised be He, saves us from their hands* (Haggadah).

Gift of Drs. Abram and Frances Pascher Kanof

82.21.1

27.

Passover Seder Plates with Dishes and Wine Cup

designed 1920s, fabricated 1975

Ludwig Yehuda Wolpert (American, born Germany, 1900-1981)

Silver: hollow-formed, pierced; glass; ebony

H overall, with cup: 9-3/4 in. (24.8 cm.);
H of plates: 4 in. (10.2 cm.); DIAM of plates: 13-3/4 in. (34.9 cm.); H of cup: 6 in. (15.2 cm.);
DIAM of cup: 2-3/4 in. (7.0 cm.);
H of dishes: 7/8 in. (2.2 cm.); DIAM of dishes: 2-7/8 in. (7.3 cm.)

Inscription (Hebrew) on cup: *I raise the cup of deliverance and invoke the name of the Lord* (Psalms 116:13).

Judaic Art Fund

76.4.6/a-j

28.

29.

30.

28.

Wine Cup for the Prophet Elijah

Late 19th century

Germany

Silver: hollow-formed, cast; die-stamped, repoussé, chased, gold-plated

H 9-3/4 in. (24.8 cm.), DIAM (rim) 4-7/16 in. (11.3 cm.)

Note: the Hebrew inscriptions identify the four sons of the traditional Passover narrative.

Gift of the Wachovia Bank and Trust Company

75.16.1

29.

Wine Cup for the Prophet Elijah

1965

Moshe Zabari (Israeli, born 1935)

Silver: hollow-formed, gold-plated; gold: appliqué

H 5-3/4 in. (14.6 cm.), D 3-9/16 in. (9.0 cm.)

Inscription (Hebrew): *Praise God in His Sanctuary* (Psalms 150:1).

Gift of Hampton Industries, in memory of its first chairman of the board, Samuel Fuchs (1888-1975)

77.3.2

30.

Hanukkah Lamp for the Synagogue

Second half of 18th century

The Netherlands

Brass: cast, turned

H 23 in. (58.4 cm.), W 23-1/4 in. (59.0 cm.)

Gift of Mr. and Mrs. Lawrence Cohen

in memory of Ned W. Cohen

78.14.1

31.

32.

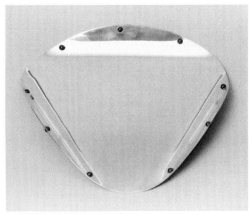

33.

31.

Hanukkah Lamp for the Home

19th century

Russia

Silver: filigree, cast

H 9-1/2 in. (24.1 cm.), W 12-1/2 in. (31.8 cm.),

D 4-7/16 in. (11.3 cm.)

Gift of Sam Ruby and Mr. and Mrs.

Richard S. Ruby

75.16.2

32.

Esther Scroll *(Megillah)* **and Case**

Mid-19th century

Austria

Silver: filigree, hollow-formed, appliqué, cast,

partially gilt; ink on parchment

H 11-1/2 in. (29.2 cm.)

Note: the scroll is inscribed with the Hebrew text

of the Book of Esther.

Gift of Drs. Abram and Frances Pascher Kanof

78.3.2

33.

Purim Plate

1966

Moshe Zabari (Israeli, born 1935)

Silver; green onyx; walnut

L 8-3/4 in. (22.2 cm.), W 8-5/8 in. (21.9 cm.)

Anonymous Gift

77.3.5

34.

35.

36.

37.

34.
Etrog (Citron) Container
1953
Ludwig Yehuda Wolpert (American, born
Germany, 1900-1981)
Silver: hollow-formed, hammered, chased
H 3-1/2 in. (8.9 cm.), W 6-3/8 in. (16.2 cm.),
D 4-3/8 in. (11.1 cm.)
Inscription (Hebrew): *The fruit of a goodly tree*
(Leviticus 23:40).
Gift of the North Carolina Association of Jewish
Men and Women
79.3.6

35.
Shofar
1751 (per inscription)
Germany
Horn: carved, pierced, engraved
L 15-1/2 in. (39.4 cm.)
Inscription (Hebrew): *Happy is the people who know*
the joyful shout; {O Lord,} they walk in the light of
Your presence (Psalms 89:16).
Gift of Mr. and Mrs. Arnold Shertz
75.16.3

36.
Woman's Spice Container in the Form of a
Floral Bouquet, for Yom Kippur Services
c. 1820
Poland
Silver: filigree; precious stones; iron
H 6-3/4 in. (17.1 cm.); W 2-5/16 in. (5.9 cm.)
Gift of Elizabeth F. Gervais-Gruen in honor of
Richard Peter Gruen
96.1.1

THE JEWISH HOME

37.
Mezuzah
1951
Ludwig Yehuda Wolpert (American, born
Germany, 1900-1981)
Silver: pierced, machine textured; plastic;
ink on parchment
H 5 in. (12.7 cm.), W 3-7/16 in. (8.7 cm.),
D 9/16 in. (1.4 cm.)
Inscription (Hebrew): *Blessed shall you be in your*
comings, and blessed shall you be in your goings
(Deuteronomy 28:6).
Gift of Dr. Ludwig Y. Wolpert in honor of the
fiftieth wedding anniversary of Drs. Abram and
Frances Pascher Kanof
81.14.1

38.

39.

40.

38.

Mezuzah

1979

Harold Rabinowitz (American, born 1939)

Silver; plastic; ink on parchment

H 2-7/8 in. (7.3 cm.), W 2-1/2 in. (6.4 cm.)

Gift of Dr. Naomi Kanof in honor of the seventy-
fifth birthday of Dr. Frances Pascher Kanof

79.3.5

39.

Book Cover with Scenes from the Bible

19th century

Italy

Silver: die-stamped, cast, chased

H 4-3/4 in. (12.1 cm.), W 3-1/4 in. (8.3 cm.),
D 1-5/16 in. (3.3 cm.)

Gift of the Kadis Family, in memory
of Isaac Kadis (1899-1979)

77.3.1a-b

40.

Alms Container for the Home

1962

Moshe Zabari (Israeli, born 1935)

Silver: hollow-formed, appliqué, sand-blasted

H 6 in. (15.2 cm.), W 2-1/16 in. (5.2 cm.),
D 2-13/16 in. (7.1 cm.)

Inscription (Hebrew): *With grace, kindness,
and compassion.*

Gift of Drs. Abram and Frances Pascher Kanof

75.33.9

The essays and commentary benefited greatly from close reading by Susan L. Braunstein, Associate Curator of Archaeology at the Jewish Museum, New York; Rebecca Martin Nagy, Associate Director of Education at the North Carolina Museum of Art; and Ann P. Roth. I am also grateful to Rabbi Jonathan Perlman and Beth Kissileff Perlman for their invaluable assistance in translating the Hebrew and Aramaic inscriptions, and to Mary Ann Scherr for identifying the various metalworking techniques. The text was capably edited by Leslie Watkins. John W. Coffey, Chair of the Curatorial Department at the North Carolina Museum of Art, first suggested this guide and encouraged my labors. His patient and loyal participation made it all possible. Most of all, I remember my wife, Dr. Frances Pascher, to whom I dedicate this guide. She was a constant source of encouragement as I made my way from medicine into Jewish art.

Abram Kanof